FANtastic Franchises

STAR WARS FRANCHISE

Kenny Abdo

Fly!
An Imprint of Abdo Zoom
abdobooks.com

abdobooks.com

Published by Abdo Zoom, a division of ABDO, P.O. Box 398166, Minneapolis, Minnesota 55439.

Printed in the United States of America, North Mankato, Minnesota.
052024
092024

Photo Credits: Alamy, Everett Collection, Getty Images, Shutterstock
Production Contributors: Kenny Abdo, Jennie Forsberg, Grace Hansen
Design Contributors: Candice Keimig, Neil Klinepier, Colleen McLaren

Library of Congress Control Number: 2023948531

Publisher's Cataloging-in-Publication Data

Names: Abdo, Kenny, author.
Title: Star Wars franchise / by Kenny Abdo
Description: Minneapolis, Minnesota : Abdo Zoom, 2025 | Series: FANtastic franchises | Includes online resources and index.
Identifiers: ISBN 9781098285593 (lib. bdg.) | ISBN 9781098286293 (ebook) | ISBN 9781098286644 (Read-to-me eBook)
Subjects: LCSH: Lucasfilm Ltd.--Juvenile literature. | Star wars (Motion picture)-Juvenile literature. | Imaginary wars and battles--Juvenile literature. | Science fiction--Juvenile literature. | Branding (Marketing)--Juvenile literature. | Popular culture--Juvenile literature.
Classification: DDC 338.768--dc23

TABLE OF CONTENTS

STAR WARS

Star Wars is a sci-fi **epic** from a galaxy far, far away and a **franchise** that is universally loved!

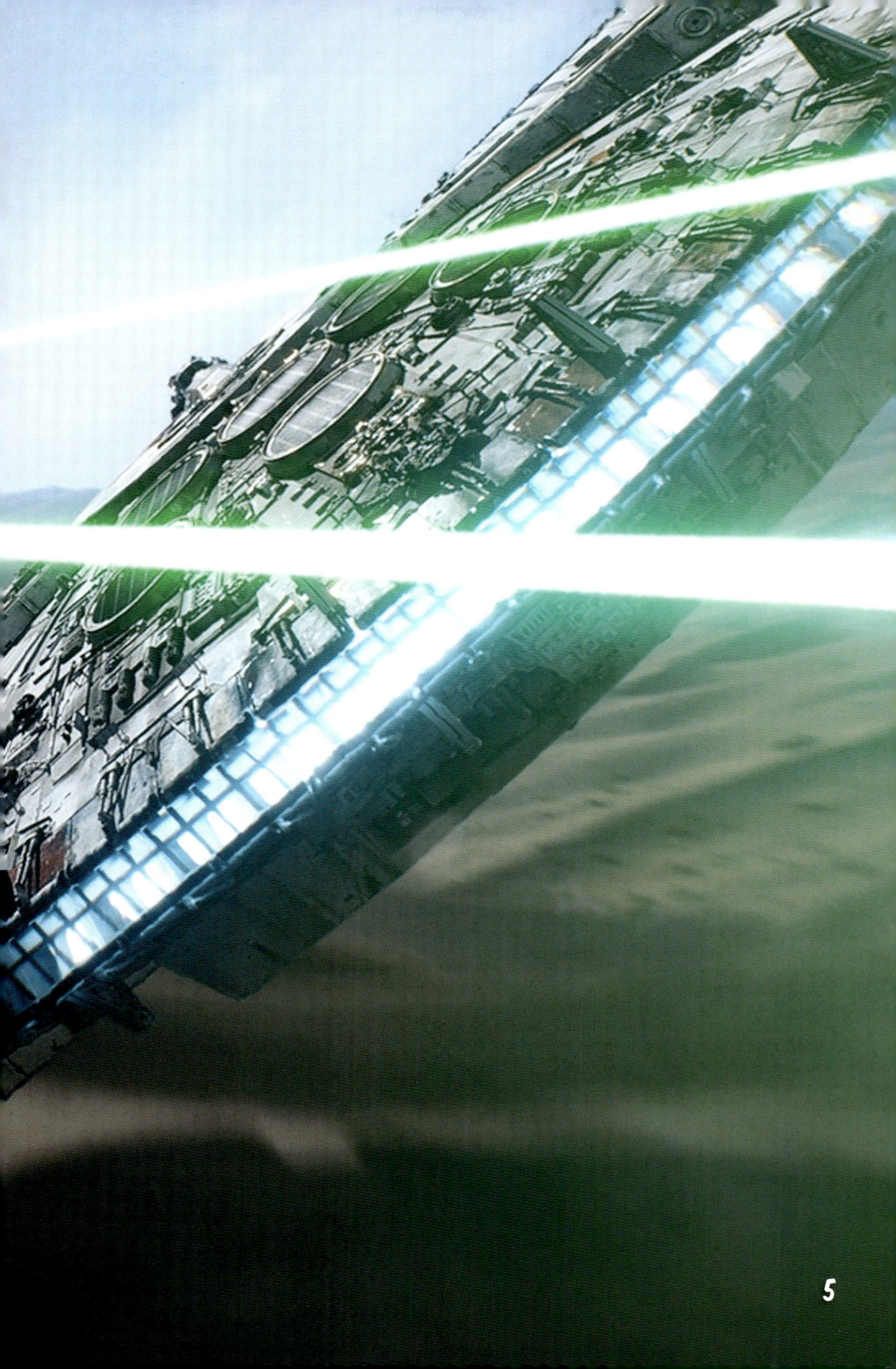

ORIGINS

George Lucas wanted to make the **space opera** of his dreams. He **pitched** *Star Wars* to many studios. The idea was rejected until 20th Century Fox finally gave him the green light!

PLEASE QUEUE HERE
FOR
10 50AM
PROGRAMME
DOORS OPEN 10 15AM

Moviegoers on May 25, 1977, were floored by what they saw. Fans and critics loved the film *Star Wars: A New Hope*. Nominated for ten **Oscars**, the movie took home six! It was the highest-**grossing** movie of the year.

THROUGH THE YEARS

Two **sequels** quickly followed. *The Empire Strikes Back* was released in 1980. It followed Luke on his quest to become a Jedi Knight. It was also revealed that (**spoiler alert**!) Darth Vader was his father.

Return of the Jedi **debuted** in 1983. It ended Lucas' Skywalker saga. Fans loved it. However, they had to say goodbye to their favorite characters. But it wouldn't be for long.

A few cartoons and radio dramas were released, expanding the Star Wars universe. And 22 years after *Star Wars* was released, Lucas surprised fans old and new.

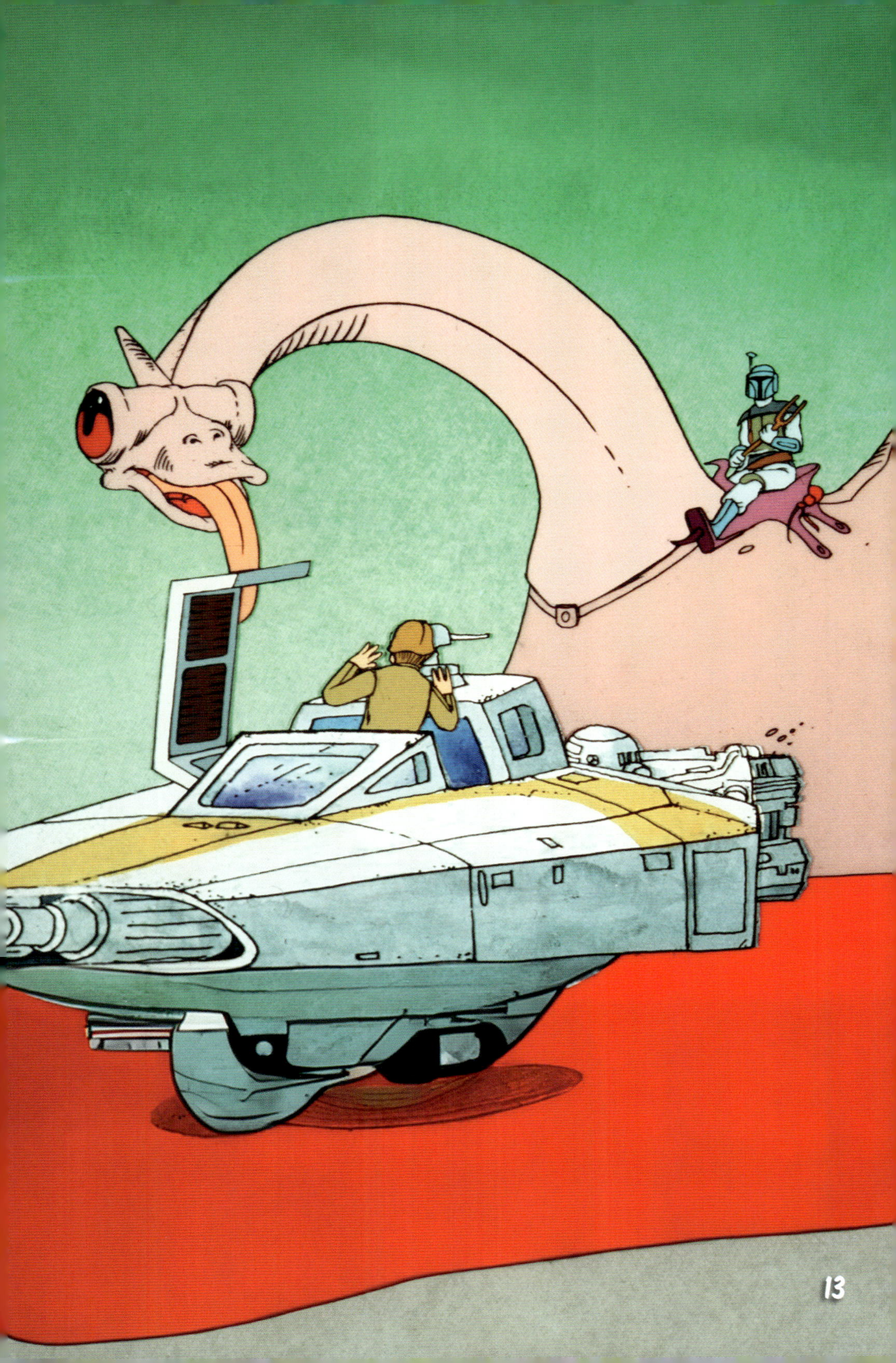

Lucas created a **prequel** series to the original. The new **trilogy** followed young Anakin Skywalker. Audiences watched him be lured to the Dark Side to become the Sith lord that the galaxy feared.

Lucas stepped away from Star Wars in 2012. Disney bought the **franchise**. Disney made a **sequel trilogy** to Lucas' original saga. The company also released the popular films *Rogue One* and *Solo*.

In 2019, Disney released *The Mandalorian*. The TV series introduced fan-favorite Grogu and became an instant hit! Disney also released series following Boba Fett, Obi-Wan Kenobi, and Cassian Andor.

Fans were welcomed into Star Wars: Galaxy's Edge that same year. At Disneyland and Disney World, guests could live out their own Star Wars adventure with rides and food, while meeting their favorite characters!

Star Wars is a merchandise titan. Action figures, video games, and bedding fill fans' homes. The **Guinness World Records** named Star Wars the most successful film merchandising **franchise** in history. The goods have earned more than $30 billion alone.

STAR WARS

FANDOM

Fans honor the Star Wars films and universe every year on May the 4th. The holiday brings fans together to celebrate the series through cosplay, movie marathons, and concerts!

Star Wars is the most successful non-superhero **franchise** ever. For a saga that takes place "a long time ago," it will be loved well into the future!

GLOSSARY

debut – a first appearance.

epic – a large-scale film that follows the journey of a hero.

franchise – a collection of related movies, TV shows, and other media in a series.

grossing – earning.

Guinness World Records – the global authority that verifies and lists records from around the world.

Oscar – another name for an Academy Award. One of several awards the Academy of Motion Picture Arts and Sciences gives annually to achievement in the movie industry.

pitch – in film, an idea for a movie.

prequel – a movie or other work that includes earlier events from an existing story.

sequel – a movie or other work that continues the story begun in an earlier work.

space opera – an epic story set in outer space.

spoiler alert – a warning that an important detail about a movie is about to be revealed.

trilogy – a movie series that has three parts.

ONLINE RESOURCES

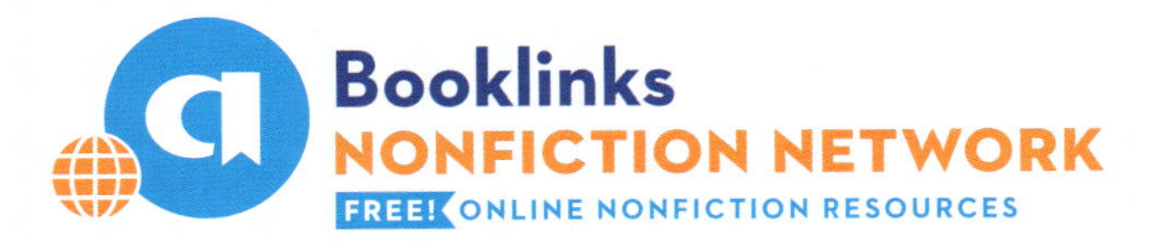

To learn more about the Star Wars franchise, please visit **abdobooklinks.com** or scan this QR code. These links are routinely monitored and updated to provide the most current information available.

INDEX